Gratitude journal for teenage girls

This journal Belongs to :

_____

UMA RAY

Introduction

Journey into this wonderful and mysterious world of teenage diaries with this specially created book that offers relaxation and balance. Each page of this gratitude journal offers you an oasis of creativity and meditation, designed to stimulate your mind and help you connect with your inner self. Each camp is meticulously crafted to guide you on a journey of relaxation and introspection.

Our book traces the elements of a day with wise drawings and illustrations, perfect for encouraging calm and mental clarity amid daily hustle and bustle. No matter your mood, and if you just want to spend your free time in a productive and relaxing way, this journal allows you to express your creativity and recharge your mental batteries in a joyful and harmony.

"Enjoy your moments of peace and reflection, and this gratitude journal will become a trusted partner in your quest for balance and inner beauty."

Thoughts, ideas, drawings.....

DATE : .... /..../....   M T W T F S S

IN THIS DAY I FELT :

_____
_____
_____
_____
_____

With every smile, I
become more
beautiful.

MY MOOD TODAY WAS:

OBJECTIVES OF THE DAY:

_____
_____
_____
_____
_____

THOUGHTS AND
IDEAS

TODAY I AM GREATFUL FOR :

_____

_____

Thoughts, ideas, drawings.....

DATE : .... /..../....　　　　M T W T F S S

IN THIS DAY I FELT :

_____
_____
_____
_____
_____

Joy comes from
simple moments.

OBJECTIVES OF THE DAY:

_____
_____
_____
_____
_____

MY MOOD TODAY WAS:

THOUGHTS AND
IDEAS

TODAY I AM GREATFUL FOR :

_____
_____

Thoughts, ideas, drawings.....

DATE : .... /..../....   M T W T F S S

IN THIS DAY I FELT :

_____
_____
_____
_____
_____

Wisdom is based on
intelligence and
common sense.

OBJECTIVES OF THE DAY:

_____
_____
_____
_____
_____

MY MOOD TODAY WAS:

THOUGHTS AND
IDEAS

TODAY I AM GREATFUL FOR :

_____

_____

_____

Thoughts, ideas, drawings.....

DATE : .... /..../....   M T W T F S S

IN THIS DAY I FELT :

_____
_____
_____
_____
_____

We don't choose our
parents, they are our
guides throughout
life.

OBJECTIVES OF THE DAY:

_____
_____
_____
_____
_____

MY MOOD TODAY WAS:

THOUGHTS AND
IDEAS

TODAY I AM GREATFUL FOR :

_____

_____

Thoughts, ideas, drawings.....

DATE : .... /..../....   M T W T F S S

IN THIS DAY I FELT :

_____
_____
_____
_____
_____

Pride of self is a lower tendency of our being, not a virtue.

OBJECTIVES OF THE DAY:

_____
_____
_____
_____

MY MOOD TODAY WAS:

THOUGHTS AND
IDEAS

TODAY I AM GREATFUL FOR :

_____

_____

_____

Thoughts, ideas, drawings.....

thought of the WEEK

Happiness and fulfillment are built from moments of self-satisfaction, of being at peace with oneself.

Objectives of the day :

_____

_____

_____

_____

An intimate place to express my
thoughts and ideas

Mood of the day :

Thoughts, ideas, drawings.....

DATE: ..../..../........ M T W T F S S

thought of the WEEK

WISDOM IS BASED ON INTELLIGENCE AND COMMON SENSE

Objectives of the day :

_____

_____

_____

_____

An intimate place to express my
            thoughts and ideas

Mood of the day :

Thoughts, ideas, drawings.....

DATE : .... /..../....   M T W T F S S

IN THIS DAY I FELT :

_____
_____
_____
_____
_____

Empathy is the best
motivation.

OBJECTIVES OF THE DAY:

_____
_____
_____
_____
_____

MY MOOD TODAY WAS:

**THOUGHTS AND
IDEAS**

TODAY I AM GREATFUL FOR :

_____

_____

Thoughts, ideas, drawings.....

DATE : .... /..../....   M T W T F S S

IN THIS DAY I FELT :

_____
_____
_____
_____
_____

Smiles will always bring a
ray of sunshine to your
soul.

MY MOOD TODAY WAS:

OBJECTIVES OF THE DAY:

_____
_____
_____
_____
_____

THOUGHTS AND
IDEAS

TODAY I AM GREATFUL FOR :

_____

_____

Thoughts, ideas, drawings.....

DATE : .... /..../....   M T W T F S S

IN THIS DAY I FELT :

_____
_____
_____
_____
_____

Common sense is made up
of words that are said and
thoughts that are not
said.

OBJECTIVES OF THE DAY:

_____
_____
_____
_____
_____

MY MOOD TODAY WAS:

THOUGHTS AND
IDEAS

TODAY I AM GREATFUL FOR :

_____
_____

Thoughts, ideas, drawings.....

DATE : .... /..../....   M T W T F S S

IN THIS DAY I FELT :
_____
_____
_____
_____
_____

The true friend is worth
loving with all his faults.

MY MOOD TODAY WAS:

OBJECTIVES OF THE DAY:
_____
_____
_____
_____
_____

THOUGHTS AND
IDEAS

TODAY I AM GREATFUL FOR :

_____

_____

Thoughts, ideas, drawings.....

DATE : .... /..../....   M T W T F S S

IN THIS DAY I FELT :

_____
_____
_____
_____

With every smile, I
become more beautiful.

MY MOOD TODAY WAS:

OBJECTIVES OF THE DAY:

_____
_____
_____
_____

THOUGHTS AND
IDEAS

TODAY I AM GREATFUL FOR :

_____

_____

Thoughts, ideas, drawings.....

thought of the WEEK

Being fair to others starts with being fair to yourself.

Objectives of the day :

_____
_____
_____
_____

An intimate place to express my
    thoughts and ideas

Mood of the day :

Thoughts, ideas, drawings.....

DATE: ..../..../........

thought of the WEEK

When you get help, be grateful.

Objectives of the day :

_____
_____
_____

_____

An intimate place to express my
    thoughts and ideas

Mood of the day :

Thoughts, ideas, drawings.....

DATE : .... /..../....   M T W T F S S

IN THIS DAY I FELT :

_____
_____
_____
_____
_____

With patience, you acquire
what you do not think.

OBJECTIVES OF THE DAY:

_____
_____
_____
_____
_____

MY MOOD TODAY WAS:

THOUGHTS AND
IDEAS

TODAY I AM GREATFUL FOR :

_____

_____

Thoughts, ideas, drawings.....

DATE : .... /..../....   M T W T F S S

IN THIS DAY I FELT :

_____
_____
_____
_____
_____

Kindness to people is truly
human behavior.

MY MOOD TODAY WAS:

OBJECTIVES OF THE DAY:

_____
_____
_____
_____
_____

THOUGHTS AND
IDEAS

TODAY I AM GREATFUL FOR :

_____

_____

Thoughts, ideas, drawings.....

DATE : .... /..../....   M T W T F S S

IN THIS DAY I FELT :
_____
_____
_____
_____

Self-esteem is built on
common sense behavior.

OBJECTIVES OF THE DAY:
_____
_____
_____
_____
_____

MY MOOD TODAY WAS:

THOUGHTS AND
IDEAS

TODAY I AM GREATFUL FOR :

_____

_____

Thoughts, ideas, drawings.....

DATE : .... /..../....　　　　M T W T F S S

IN THIS DAY I FELT :

_____
_____
_____
_____

With every smile, I become
more beautiful.

OBJECTIVES OF THE DAY:

_____
_____
_____
_____
_____

MY MOOD TODAY WAS:

THOUGHTS AND
IDEAS

TODAY I AM GREATFUL FOR :

_____

_____

_____

Thoughts, ideas, drawings.....

DATE : .... /..../....   M T W T F S S

IN THIS DAY I FELT :
_____
_____
_____
_____
_____

Faith well healed brings the
rose in our hearts to bloom.

OBJECTIVES OF THE DAY:
_____
_____
_____
_____
_____

MY MOOD TODAY WAS:

THOUGHTS AND
IDEAS

TODAY I AM GREATFUL FOR :

_____

_____

Thoughts, ideas, drawings.....

thought of the WEEK

Creativity is acquired with every moment of practice.

Objectives of the day :

_____
_____
_____
_____

An intimate place to express my
thoughts and ideas

Mood of the day :

Thoughts, ideas, drawings.....

DATE: ..../..../........   M T W T F S S

thought of the WEEK

Grief does not bring benefits in the long run, it digs into the soul of the human being forming pits that are hard to fill.

Objectives of the day :

_____

_____

_____

_____

An intimate place to express my
    thoughts and ideas

Mood of the day :

Thoughts, ideas, drawings.....

DATE : .... /..../....   M T W T F S S

IN THIS DAY I FELT :

_____
_____
_____
_____
_____

A smile in the morning is like a glass of clean spring water.

MY MOOD TODAY WAS:

OBJECTIVES OF THE DAY:

_____
_____
_____
_____

THOUGHTS AND
IDEAS

TODAY I AM GREATFUL FOR :

_____

_____

Thoughts, ideas, drawings.....

DATE : …. /…./….   M T W T F S S

IN THIS DAY I FELT :

_____
_____
_____
_____
_____

Exterior cleaning starts
with interior cleaning

OBJECTIVES OF THE DAY:

_____
_____
_____
_____
_____

MY MOOD TODAY WAS:

**THOUGHTS AND
IDEAS**

TODAY I AM GREATFUL FOR :

_____

_____

Thoughts, ideas, drawings.....

DATE : .... /..../....

M T W T F S S

IN THIS DAY I FELT :

_____
_____
_____
_____
_____

In everything you want to do well, be persistent.

MY MOOD TODAY WAS:

OBJECTIVES OF THE DAY:

_____
_____
_____
_____
_____

THOUGHTS AND
IDEAS

TODAY I AM GREATFUL FOR :

_____

_____

Thoughts, ideas, drawings.....

DATE : .... /..../....

M T W T F S S

IN THIS DAY I FELT :

_____
_____
_____
_____
_____

Healthy maturity of mind grows with common sense and wisdom.

MY MOOD TODAY WAS.

OBJECTIVES OF THE DAY:

_____
_____
_____
_____
_____

THOUGHTS AND IDEAS

TODAY I AM GREATFUL FOR :

_____

_____

Thoughts, ideas, drawings.....

DATE : .... /..../....   M T W T F S S

IN THIS DAY I FELT :

_____
_____
_____
_____
_____

Being good is not the same
as being stupid.

MY MOOD TODAY WAS:

OBJECTIVES OF THE DAY:

_____
_____
_____
_____

THOUGHTS AND
IDEAS

TODAY I AM GREATFUL FOR :

_____

_____

_____

Thoughts, ideas, drawings.....

thought of the WEEK

The tree is watered from childhood every day, so man is educated from childhood in common sense, both having verticality in maturity.

Objectives of the day :

_____
_____
_____
_____

An intimate place to express my
    thoughts and ideas

Mood of the day :

Thoughts, ideas, drawings.....

DATE: ..../..../........   M T W T F S S

thought of the WEEK

The most precious gold is respect and help for those around you, which starts with self-respect.

Objectives of the day :

_____
_____
_____
_____

An intimate place to express my
thoughts and ideas

Mood of the day :

Thoughts, ideas, drawings.....

DATE : .... /..../....   M T W T F S S

IN THIS DAY I FELT :
_____
_____
_____
_____
_____

Goodness resides in the
soul, not in the thought.

OBJECTIVES OF THE DAY:
_____
_____
_____
_____
_____

MY MOOD TODAY WAS:

THOUGHTS AND
IDEAS

TODAY I AM GREATFUL FOR :

_____

_____

Thoughts, ideas, drawings.....

DATE : .... /..../....   M T W T F S S

IN THIS DAY I FELT :

_____
_____
_____
_____
_____

I am full of gratitude
for everything that
life has given me so
far.

MY MOOD TODAY WAS:

OBJECTIVES OF THE DAY:

_____
_____
_____
_____

THOUGHTS AND
IDEAS

TODAY I AM GREATFUL FOR :

_____

_____

Thoughts, ideas, drawings.....

DATE : .... /..../....   M T W T F S S

IN THIS DAY I FELT :
_____
_____
_____
_____
_____

Wisdom is based on
intelligence and common
sense.

MY MOOD TODAY WAS:

OBJECTIVES OF THE DAY:
_____
_____
_____
_____
_____

THOUGHTS AND
IDEAS

TODAY I AM GREATFUL FOR :

_____

_____

Thoughts, ideas, drawings.....

DATE : .... /..../....   M T W T F S S

IN THIS DAY I FELT :

_____
_____
_____
_____
_____

We don't choose our
parents, they are our
guides throughout life.

MY MOOD TODAY WAS:

OBJECTIVES OF THE DAY:

_____
_____
_____
_____
_____

THOUGHTS AND
IDEAS

TODAY I AM GREATFUL FOR :

_____
_____

Thoughts, ideas, drawings.....

DATE : .... /..../....   M T W T F S S

IN THIS DAY I FELT :
_____
_____
_____
_____
_____

The overwhelming pleasure
is always present when we
know how to surround
ourselves with wonderful
people whom we love.

MY MOOD TODAY WAS:

OBJECTIVES OF THE DAY:
_____
_____
_____
_____
_____

THOUGHTS AND
IDEAS

TODAY I AM GREATFUL FOR :

_____

_____

Thoughts, ideas, drawings.....

thought of the WEEK

Happiness and fulfillment are built from moments of self-satisfaction, of being at peace with oneself.

Objectives of the day :

_____
_____
_____
_____

An intimate place to express my
    thoughts and ideas

Mood of the day :

Thoughts, ideas, drawings.....

DATE: ..../..../........

M T W T F S S

thought of the WEEK

WISDOM IS BASED ON INTELLIGENCE AND COMMON SENSE

Objectives of the day :

_____

_____

_____

_____

An intimate place to express my
thoughts and ideas

Mood of the day :

Thoughts, ideas, drawings.....

DATE : .... /..../....   M T W T F S S

IN THIS DAY I FELT :
_____
_____
_____
_____
_____

Take the time to make real friends to get through life more easily.

OBJECTIVES OF THE DAY:
_____
_____
_____
_____
_____

MY MOOD TODAY WAS:

THOUGHTS AND
IDEAS

TODAY I AM GREATFUL FOR :

_____

_____

Thoughts, ideas, drawings.....

DATE : .... /..../....   M T W T F S S

IN THIS DAY I FELT :

_____
_____
_____
_____
_____

A smile in the morning is like a glass of clean spring water.

MY MOOD TODAY WAS:

OBJECTIVES OF THE DAY:

_____
_____
_____
_____
_____

THOUGHTS AND
IDEAS

TODAY I AM GREATFUL FOR :

_____

_____

Thoughts, ideas, drawings.....

DATE : .... /..../....   M T W T F S S

IN THIS DAY I FELT :
_____
_____
_____
_____
_____

With every smile, I become
more beautiful.

MY MOOD TODAY WAS:

OBJECTIVES OF THE DAY:
_____
_____
_____
_____
_____

THOUGHTS AND
IDEAS

TODAY I AM GREATFUL FOR :

_____

_____

Thoughts, ideas, drawings.....

DATE : .... /..../....   M T W T F S S

IN THIS DAY I FELT :

_____
_____
_____
_____
_____

Wisdom is based on
intelligence and common
sense.

OBJECTIVES OF THE DAY:

_____
_____
_____
_____
_____

MY MOOD TODAY WAS:

THOUGHTS AND
IDEAS

TODAY I AM GREATFUL FOR :

_____

_____

Thoughts, ideas, drawings.....

DATE : .... /..../....   M T W T F S S

IN THIS DAY I FELT :
_____
_____
_____
_____
_____

True love is the only flower
that grows and blooms at
any time, without the help
of the seasons.

MY MOOD TODAY WAS:

OBJECTIVES OF THE DAY:
_____
_____
_____
_____
_____

THOUGHTS AND
    IDEAS

TODAY I AM GREATFUL FOR :

_____
_____
_____

Thoughts, ideas, drawings.....

thought of the WEEK

Happiness and fulfillment are built from moments of self-satisfaction, of being at peace with oneself.

Objectives of the day :

_____

_____

_____

_____

An intimate place to express my
thoughts and ideas

Mood of the day :

Thoughts, ideas, drawings.....

DATE: ..../..../........   M T W T F S S

thought of the WEEK

WISDOM IS BASED ON INTELLIGENCE AND COMMON SENSE

Objectives of the day :

_____

_____

_____

_____

An intimate place to express my
        thoughts and ideas

Mood of the day :

Thoughts, ideas, drawings.....

DATE : .... /..../....   M T W T F S S

IN THIS DAY I FELT :

_____
_____
_____
_____
_____

Patience gives rise to hope
for a better future.

MY MOOD TODAY WAS:

OBJECTIVES OF THE DAY:

_____
_____
_____
_____
_____

**THOUGHTS AND
IDEAS**

TODAY I AM GREATFUL FOR :

_____
_____

Thoughts, ideas, drawings.....

DATE : .... /..../....   M T W T F S S

IN THIS DAY I FELT :

_____
_____
_____
_____
_____

We don't choose our
parents, they are our
guides throughout life.

OBJECTIVES OF THE DAY:

_____
_____
_____
_____
_____

MY MOOD TODAY WAS:

THOUGHTS AND
    IDEAS

TODAY I AM GREATFUL FOR :

_____

_____

Thoughts, ideas, drawings.....

DATE : .... /..../....   M T W T F S S

IN THIS DAY I FELT :
_____
_____
_____
_____
_____

A smile in the morning is like a glass of clean spring water.

MY MOOD TODAY WAS:

OBJECTIVES OF THE DAY:
_____
_____
_____
_____
_____

THOUGHTS AND IDEAS

TODAY I AM GREATFUL FOR :

_____

_____

_____

Thoughts, ideas, drawings.....

DATE : .... /..../....   M T W T F S S

IN THIS DAY I FELT :

_____
_____
_____
_____
_____

All the sincere smiles you
send to other people always
come back to you and fill
you with joy.

MY MOOD TODAY WAS:

OBJECTIVES OF THE DAY:

_____
_____
_____
_____
_____

THOUGHTS AND
IDEAS

TODAY I AM GREATFUL FOR :

_____
_____

Thoughts, ideas, drawings.....

DATE : .... /..../....   M T W T F S S

IN THIS DAY I FELT :

_____
_____
_____
_____

With every smile, I become
more beautiful.

OBJECTIVES OF THE DAY:

_____
_____
_____
_____

MY MOOD TODAY WAS:

THOUGHTS AND
IDEAS

TODAY I AM GREATFUL FOR :

_____

_____

Thoughts, ideas, drawings.....

thought of the WEEK

Happiness and fulfillment are built from moments of self-satisfaction, of being at peace with oneself.

Objectives of the day :

_____

_____

_____

_____

An intimate place to express my
    thoughts and ideas

Mood of the day :

Thoughts, ideas, drawings.....

DATE: ..../..../........   M T W T F S S

thought of the WEEK

WISDOM IS BASED ON INTELLIGENCE AND COMMON SENSE

Objectives of the day :

_____
_____
_____
_____

An intimate place to express my
    thoughts and ideas

Mood of the day :

Thoughts, ideas, drawings.....

DATE : .... /..../....   M T W T F S S

IN THIS DAY I FELT :

_____
_____
_____
_____
_____

In everything you want to
do well, be persistent.

OBJECTIVES OF THE DAY:

_____
_____
_____
_____
_____

MY MOOD TODAY WAS:

THOUGHTS AND
IDEAS

TODAY I AM GREATFUL FOR :

_____

_____

Thoughts, ideas, drawings.....

DATE : .... /..../....   M T W T F S S

IN THIS DAY I FELT :

_____
_____
_____
_____
_____

Common sense is made up of
words that are said and
thoughts that are not said.

MY MOOD TODAY WAS:

OBJECTIVES OF THE DAY:

_____
_____
_____
_____
_____

THOUGHTS AND
IDEAS

TODAY I AM GREATFUL FOR :

_____

_____

105

Thoughts, ideas, drawings.....

DATE : .... /..../....   M T W T F S S

IN THIS DAY I FELT :

_____
_____
_____
_____
_____

With patience, you acquire
what you do not think.

OBJECTIVES OF THE DAY:

_____
_____
_____
_____

MY MOOD TODAY WAS:

THOUGHTS AND
     IDEAS

TODAY I AM GREATFUL FOR :

_____

_____

Thoughts, ideas, drawings.....

DATE : .... /..../....   M T W T F S S

IN THIS DAY I FELT :

_____
_____
_____
_____
_____

The true friend is worth
loving with all his faults.

OBJECTIVES OF THE DAY:

_____
_____
_____
_____
_____

MY MOOD TODAY WAS:

THOUGHTS AND
IDEAS

TODAY I AM GREATFUL FOR :

_____

_____

_____

Thoughts, ideas, drawings.....

DATE : .... /..../....   M T W T F S S

IN THIS DAY I FELT :
_____
_____
_____
_____
_____

Smiles will always bring a
ray of sunshine to your soul.

MY MOOD TODAY WAS:

OBJECTIVES OF THE DAY:
_____
_____
_____
_____
_____

THOUGHTS AND
IDEAS

TODAY I AM GREATFUL FOR :

_____

_____

_____

Thoughts, ideas, drawings.....

DATE: ..../..../........

M T W T F S S

thought of the WEEK

WISDOM IS BASED ON INTELLIGENCE AND COMMON SENSE

Objectives of the day :

_____

_____

_____

_____

An intimate place to express my
    thoughts and ideas

Mood of the day :

Thoughts, ideas, drawings.....

DATE: ..../..../........   M T W T F S S

thought of the WEEK

WISDOM IS BASED ON INTELLIGENCE AND COMMON SENSE

Objectives of the day :

_____

_____

_____

_____

An intimate place to express my
thoughts and ideas

Mood of the day :

Thank you !

As the author of this gratitude journal, I wanted to take a moment to express my gratitude for making it happen.

It gives us great joy to know that our small family company has been a part of your life.

In our company we create from heart and soul, unique coloring books, journals, mandala books, quality, that inspire and center human beings.

If you enjoyed this gratitude journal and found it to be a source of joy, encouragement, and growth, please leave a review on Amazon. Your words have immense power and can make a significant impact on our small business. Your support will not only help us reach more people, but also inspire us to keep creating meaningful books.

We understand that leaving a review may seem like a small action, but it means a lot to us. Your support will enable us to continue to produce quality books that touch the lives of our peers and feed their imaginations.

If you have suggestions for improvement, you can contact us at our email address:
uma.ray3011@gmail.com

With deep appreciation,
Uma Ray

Made in the USA
Monee, IL
23 September 2024